This is Where I Live Now

Kimmy Joy

BookLeaf Publishing

India | USA | UK

Presentation by *BookLeaf Publishing*

Web: www.bookleafpub.com

E-mail: info@bookleafpub.com

ISBN: 9789358311815

First edition 2023

For Nathaniel, obviously.

ACKNOWLEDGEMENT

I would like to thank Leah Joy, who also did this poetry challenge. You should snag a copy of her 21-day-challenge book, One Oh One, as her work is splendid.

Thanks are also due to Don Hough, who provided the last-minute push of encouragement I needed to finish strong.

As always and for everything, I thank Declan Maher.

PREFACE

God, I hope nobody is reading this.

No, really. It feels odd writing this preface, knowing that anyone who's reading this book has already ostensibly spent money to do so, and it is so thoroughly not the book that I meant to write, and I am unhappy submitting the form to confirm publication, but then again, I spent the money to sign up for this weird little stunt and I'm trying to actually follow through on the projects I start.

So, in case you missed why this book exists: I saw a targeted ad on Facebook for a challenge where you write 21 poems in 21 days and BookLeaf makes a cute little chapbook. I saw this roughly a week before moving to Indiana to live with my new boyfriend and thought "I bet I'll have a lot to write about." And I did, but...

It's only fair for me to admit that I failed this challenge. The point was to write a poem every day. Instead, something happened around day 8 that took the wind out of my sails so thoroughly that I ended up writing two-thirds of the book in the last week, which isn't the spirit of the thing, but eh. We do what we can.

If you've purchased a copy of this, I owe you a drink. Clearly you love me more than I love myself at the moment. But we're working on that.

KJ

too soon

there are a few things you should know:

canada is burning. all week
i stared down a smoky skyline
as it faded into obscurity. i'm leaving
tonight and this morning
i couldn't see the buildings
from the bridge. the towers
did not say goodbye.

i knew him for 23 years
before seeing his face
like a portentous thunderclap.
he yoyoed between boot and mitten
for two months before i threw
the towel like a gauntlet and
quit my job. i loved being
in his passenger seat
on flat roads where i felt like
roadkill.

the girls at work drank my success
for hours after i left the party. all of them
are hung over on my last day. i pack my things
slowly. leave the snacks behind,

give the fidget toys away. everyone
is looking for an excuse.

ashley told me she was worried.
this was weeks ago, she said
it seemed too soon to go.
it's hard to tell a stranger
that this was me taking things slow.
never have i ever
given a 30-day notice.
mostly it's been trash bags
in the back of someone's car.

mostly it's been quick moves,
the way i play chess, no forethought.
the knight dives in his bent path
simply because the way was open.
i castle without understanding
why people castle.

i ordered a book on chess for beginners.
we played to a draw on our second date.

a tree, portrait

before root's tangle
and the scrape of diseased bark
our soil is baked hard
by the sun's kilnfire
and underneath that even
the water is off in some way
perhaps poison, heavy metals
leaching into the table

at midday we walked the midway
two laps of rainbow rides
and lemon crushes
i drank the humidity without
breathing and we slid past
aisles of your childhood
memories molded from plastic
and wrapped in plastic

i have written too many words about being tired.
there is no fear in love
but surely there is exhaustion.

nevermind

the produce section is a zoo
and all of the baby spinach
fondled to rot. how can I speak
loudly enough to be heard? is it
that I use words too
gently? the seer told me
I'm an acetylene torch. It's still
a form of softness, you see.

after all of these years
lifting weights the emergency
alert siren morphs me into
a tiny girl hiding in the stale air
under my grandmother's mattress.
did I tell you I'm deathly afraid
of tornadoes? did I tell you
I have eaten fire professionally?

good listeners with rough hands
are my favorite kind of people.

quartet

it's just you and me and the dog
and all of your fucking neighbors
with their goddamn fireworks.

dog too fat, too stoned
to jump on bed. dog
too dumb to use new dog bed.
dog scared shitless. no poop
in days. I'm scared too.

as we were drifting off
someone fired, like, a cannon
just outside his bedroom
and sent sparklers of rage
through my skull. fireworks
are legal here. is arson?
a house might burn, right,
if it's owner is a FUCKING DUMBASS
who keeps explosives around
and has no regard for the sleeping
hours of normal people.

nobody says "it's a bad day
for proprioception" but
on my shaky limbs I've managed

to unpack boxes, cook frittata
and soup, and help your neighbors
catch their rambunctious chihuahua.
it's a bad day to be in motion,
it's a bad day if you're a dog,
it's a bad day for feng shui,
but a very good day
to eat cake in bed.

pity I don't have any cake.

ode to jello shots

there is a drunk ten year old
three feet from me
who is not actually ten years old
but says that they are ten years old
and
I don't understand the world I live in.

here's what I do understand. one
cup of water, boil, leave it on
the stove and dissolve a box
of jello, the larger box, berry
blue and when it's totally dissolved
you add a cup of bottom shelf
vodka and pour into a casserole
dish and leave in the fridge
overnight and the next day
do it again but with strawberry.

let the record show:
the most fuck-you way to drink
is jello shots

I want to make everyone happy,
even the ones I don't understand.
I'm very tired. I'm learning all

of the time. And it's stupid
that I feel wrong at times like
this, watching videogamevideos
against my will with children who
are legal in body. I have asked
so many questions over the past
few days. am I confused or
simply afraid of being judged?

I do like this holiday.
I like celebrating saying
"fuck you."

if I could demand
that everyone around me
would treat me as a certain age
which would I pick?
not ten, certainly –
maybe seventeen?
not even a child, really.
just the age where I really, really wish
I'd learned to say "fuck you."

but it wasn't
until my thirties
that I learned
to make
jello shots

untitled

One day, it all fell apart.

I wrote nothing. I took a nap.
I did not look
for a job. I woke up
with a hole so deep
I could bury you in it
and I haven't been in the light
since. Small glimmers
come through, at the lake,
with a drink in my hand,
but nothing to follow
as far as I must walk.

You are running out ahead,
breathing fresh clean air.
I can feel your heart gasp
blood into every vein,
every capillary shouts its name
out loud, one-two, one-two.

You are running out
ahead.

maybe it's better this way

a snail does not make its shell
overnight. it happens slowly,
layers built, a spiral accruing,
and this is how we say
goodbye, no? Yes, yes it is.

excruciatingly slow and dextrous
I will block you out. your radiation
and angelic possession reception
projection description progression
will not assail me. I have learned
to shut down my heart. My heart!
is worth more empty than loved
by you or me or anyone else.

I have learned to construct it all
one layer at a time: see here, you
could dig deep, if you want, like I
said, like splitting firewood, like
tearing lace, like diving into a pool
of murky emerald. we both know
how deep and wide, we sang it
in church countless times. You

were everything

tilted

the world went off-goddamn axis
at some point it's fully been
two weeks since any ink
touched my page and
i'd said that i would
write at least one
more poem
every fuck
ing day
and i
am
so

sad

resume

ross dress for less hasn't called me back
nobody has really but that one bothers me
for reasons i can't quite fathom myself
i can feel my light dim with every application
the ocean becomes less fathomable
taking points from the singlespaced
page describing the full depth and breadth
of what really matters about me there's
just not all that much i suppose and
it's been a couple of weeks since
i showed up to the office or did anything
other than dishes and laundry but
like the name of the page i guess
it's time to try again, to continue, to
resume

tickertape

hard to blame you for the cuts, darling —
we both know i was bleeding on that day,
my hair all matted from the rain, lost dog
cowering kicked on your doorstep. hard
to blame you when these are scalpel cuts
and you're a large mallet. no, you wouldn't
know where to put a blade, not unless i
went ahead and showed you. far too hard
to point fingers and they're missing, too,
anyway. you dashed to the store and bought
five hundred rolls of gauze and threw them
around the house like i'd returned from war
victorious instead of defeated. you threw
a parade and a feast to follow and i followed
and i tried to follow the swaths of white
hanging from the ceiling fans, windowpanes,
crown molding, stuck in the icemaker, but
i could not find the end. perhaps i didn't
want to find it. instead i sat on the other
side of the room and asked you how much
money you spent at the pharmacy, my love.

we both promised

to be honest
to be faithful
to correct each other's spelling
to never eat a dish that tastes bad
        (but it's okay if it makes you sick,
          as long as it tastes good)
to go on long drives
to walk the dog, when we have the energy
to make each other laugh
to not get angry when our spelling is corrected
        (or at least to be graceful in our
anger)
to care
to go to work
to sleep enough, if we can
to be honest
        (again — it's never bad to say things
twice)
to repeat ourselves if necessary
to listen
to listen
to listen
to listen
to listen
to listen

and you listened

when it didn't matter, and broke windows
when it did. we keep talking about the
drunk ten year old in the room because
somehow a drunk ten year old can grow
bigger than an elephant. i am not afraid
to speak: he who has ears, let him hear.

when i was fourteen i climbed up into
wesley's tree to have a lonely place to cry
about love but what i really wanted was
to be seen, face pressed into the bark,
deep as igneous rock, but i was always
sand and shallow men bury only their feet.

but i was thinking about him and how
gently he was able to speak through fire.
i never had a steely core, i melt clear
and cure brittle. i never wanted to be
alone and was certain to my bones that
i'd be unwanted to my sorry grave.
it's good to be wrong sometimes. sometimes.

there's glass all over the floor, so i wear
boots indoors and try to keep from bleeding
on anything you own that is white. i'm sorry
i don't sound happy. it's just that my heart
is broken.

Dear Nathan

It's weird that this will end up in print. When I
signed up for this "write a chapbook gradually
over the course of 21 days" stunt, I thought
about being on the precipice of a huge life
change and how writing something each day
about whatever happened on that day might be a
fun challenge and something that would be
interesting for other people to read. I thought
"surely there will be some funny little stories,
some poignant moments—" god knows there's
been enough of them between us to fill a book
already. I imagined poems about touching
everything you own and deciding what stays and
what goes, poems about crossing state lines,
about new love and new adventures in a new
place, about small-town boredom, about the
haunted playground factory, about the turmoil of
leaving my old life breaking into bliss and
brilliance and peace.

And then we had that fight. You know the one.

It's not exactly that it sucked all of the wind out
of my sails, although it kind of did, and it's not
exactly that it crushed my desire to write poetry,

although it kind of did, and it's not that I haven't
been happy ever since, although I kind of
haven't — it's that everything between us since
then has felt intensely private, and when I sit
down to write it, it doesn't feel right.

I wanted to include this piece for you to
understand the sadness, because the sadness isn't
really about the fight itself. The sadness is
because after that night, I felt like I couldn't talk
about you as much anymore. Because what if…?
Because what would my friends say if they
knew…? Because how can I be thinking
about…? and poetry lives in those ellipses, and
so do you. And it wouldn't be fair to write the
ellipses, to show us, you, in our, your, worst
light. And of course there was still happiness:
remember that night when…? but those ellipses
are private in their own way, and quiet happiness
curled up with someone you love is the most
beautifully banal thing in the world and
extremely difficult to write a good poem about.

Still, I guess, I'll try.

Love, KJ

ode to snoring

if you wanna be my lover
you gotta get a deviated septum
or a prominent soft palate
or maybe sleep apnea
or just be sorta squishy
whichever path you choose
i doubt i could ever truly love
a silent sleeper

it's not soothing my dreams splinter
and tear to the rhythm of your
hacksaw symphony i complain
i nudge i make you roll
over and curl up close
face pressed between shoulders
one hand on your heart
the other in your hair

i am Big Spoon i have
always been Big Spoon i melt
the hardest coldest ice
sculptures of men into slush
with a breath at the back
of the neck the strongest
men sleep soundest

when they feel protected
held shrinkrayed into
tininess and kept
in my softest pocket

o weary one find rest in my arms
when the night terrors come
i will remind you of what's real

rarity

as children we cannot read the map
of our own hearts and feelings
are a language parsed by the grownups
the unnameability and unfamiliarity
of emotions becomes part
of the emotion itself

as adults we lose this
newness-and-confusion with
milk teeth and is it too banal
or inaccurate to say innocence
feelings come with names
and a sense of recognition

nobody's made me feel
this way before means i have
tasted these flavors separately
never in the specific cocktail
mixed and poured by you

all that being said
tell it to me as true as you can
has anyone made you feel
this way before?

sleeping alone pt ii

sitcom laughs burble through
the crack under the door and
slither toward the bed
where i am
carbon dating the sob
caught in my chest
revealed by anger's
radioactive glow too old
to have lodged there during
our battle it sits years deep
and i want to chip the schist
with a pickaxe and feed you
this fossilized sadness
or perhaps simply hand it over
so you can press it
between pages of your book
like a flower.

compliance

to you and you alone i will confess the full
extent of my failure:

compliance is a wrought iron tool. first, pry me
open
poke and prod for truth, you could leave a few
bruises
for good measure. compliance is a river and you
could
hang something heavy round my neck, throw me
in
and watch as i sink into its current forever. it's
not
the first good time with which i have been aptly
threatened but it might be the best. i wish you
could
crack open this ol skull and trace the synaptic
pathways
to see my morning sensitivity and exactly how
crazy i am
for you. compliance is a toyota corolla, silver,
and you
could hit the gas and run me down fast enough
that

nobody would catch your license plate number.
compliance
is my boyfriend, compliance is a god.
compliance is
a taylor swift song and you're singing along in
the kitchen.
compliance is the moral of the fable i heard so
many times,
a holy number of times, and i spat the words at
an artist
with a needle and asked him to ink it so deep
and hidden
that you will bury it with me when i've drowned
myself.

to you and you alone i will confess the full
extent of my failure:

this space intentionally left blank.

lovers in a dangerous time

do we hold each other so closely
because when we were babies
our parents filled our little milk bottles
with stories of the end times?
because when we were old enough
we tried to believe the apocalypse
was simply a story written to open
us and scoop out our agency,
only to find that the world is indeed
ending in fire and smoke
and pandemics and famine,
drug shortages, polarized politics,
mass shootings, phone addiction,
crises of faith and literacy, and
babel's miscommunication?
how much of this runs through you
when your fingers graze an artery?
you know this fear is in my blood.
can you feel it in my pulse?
do you taste it on my teeth?

what are you wearing to the apocalypse

it's flat fuck friday, you fucking losers.
roll the tape, i am rough like an alligator.
if it was wednesday i'd find some bad
taxidermy to show you. you're in work-
wear, i'm still in my tony soprano pants
with all the lights off going blind from
the blank page in front of me. hungry.
starving actually, unappetized by the
feast at my elbow. i've done my best
to make my body disappear over time.

do we fight because the world is ending
and we can't fight the end times? i keep
trying to pray, dialtone desperate
and devoid of grace. i am sorry
i showed up fullhearted
and emptyhanded.

this is all i have:
flannel and cotton, satin shirts,
the peekaboo dress i wore to the party
with the drunk ten-year-old. cheap
lace like sandpaper. one sock at a time,
one nice brassiere. lift me up,
pray for me, kiss me hard.

untilted

the birdsongs outside are unfamiliar
but i have kenn's book to teach me about
this new landscape. shame everything
is backlit and my glasses aren't enough.
all i see is shapes, shapes against the sun,
shapes in the gloomy clouds, shape of
me curled into your bedsheets. fingers
reshaped by dishwater. words shaped
and silenced by both of us. i beg you
sing for me and the sound is unfamiliar.

coded exit

it's apologies all around for the
feverish apples i've offered. we formed a
band yesterday; just booked the farewell world
tour. pills for the pain and movies for the pain as
well.
i dipped my cup into the swamp and came up far
too dry.
did you hear, canada's burning? would have
liked to see it once
more. cross toronto off the tour schedule, strike
burning love
from the setlist. have your people call my
people. dean
young has answered more prayers than his
phone
plan allows. i'm no longer young but still
beautiful
and that's the last time you'll hear me admit
either of those things. if my longlost flame
dies from poisoned air or we burn to
death in a newfound flame i will
throw bricks until my skin
blisters and tears
into arrows
and——-